ON THE DEATH OF MANUEL II

John Bessarion,
Cardinal-Archbishop of Nicaea

Translated by: D.P. Curtin

Dalcassian Publishing Company

Copyright @ 2010 Dalcassian Publishing Company

All rights reserved. No part of this publication may be reproduced, distributed, or transmitted in any form or by any means, including photocopying, recording, or other electronic or mechanical methods, without the prior written permission of the publisher, except in the case of brief quotations embodied in critical reviews and certain other non-commercial uses permitted by copyright law. For permission request, write to Dalcassian Publishing Company at dalcassianpublishing at gmail.com

ISBN: 979-8-8691-6807-8 (Paperback)

Library of Congress Control Number:
Author: Curtin, D.P. (1985-)

Printed by Ingram Content Group, 1 Ingram Blvd, La Vergne, Tennessee

First printing edition 2010.

ON THE DEATH OF MANUEL II

ON THE DEATH OF MANUEL II

If sometimes it is right to weep, and to establish a bitter association of song and sorrow, I do not see that the time can be better adapted to this matter than the present, in which whatever joy, pleasure, and pleasure there was, has been taken away and extinguished, and instead of these, sorrow and misery have succeeded. , moaning What more consolation can there be for us now, than the hope of a better fortune, as a remedy for so much unhappiness? Now let the world be cut off, let all change their clothes, all assume a mournful attitude, and with one voice deplore so great a calamity. For we have not done a mean loss, nor have we suffered an evil for which a remedy can be applied. The divine emperor, the glory of the whole world, has suddenly been taken away from us; who, by the gift of a kind of Providence, had taken the helm of things, in order to provide tranquility, rest, and happiness to all; that he might be the common father of all; that human affairs may flourish with dignity and glory. Already all fortune has changed: everything is slipping for the worse and things are returning to their former state. Wretched me! How much damage was done by the destruction of one man! He has gone and departed from life: he has left us nothing but sighs, and mourning, and tears. He took away from us all joy, he took away happiness, he took away freedom, and what was most beautiful of all, he took away himself. Alas! who is so constant, or rather hard, and truly diamond-like, that he can restrain himself from tears; who is not moved both in mind and in horror with his whole body; who does not search for the deceased, and with a groan, if possible, strive to bring him back to life? Why did you fly from us so suddenly, most pious emperor? Why didn't you want to stay with us longer? Why should the kingdom of Rome no longer enjoy the concert of your virtues? You have taken all care of us up to now, and so that we may live safe and experienced in labor, you alone have always worked best. All the peoples testify to this; all the provinces bear witness; all the earth and all the seas bear witness. But now you are gone, taking all your good things with you. What joy can we have in life without you? For we are all seen to be dead and reduced to nothing. Alas, the sun, who surveys the works of the world with shining rays! How unlucky and unhappy you have made this day bright for us! Alas! What a bitter, unworthy, and pitiful spectacle you yourself saw! It would certainly have been better to have left us wandering beneath the earth, in perpetual darkness, than to illuminate the higher regions with the brightness of your rays, so that with unhappy eyes we might see this bust of the royal body, which had so many labors, so many vigils, and so many dangers for us had often undergone. Oh, what rays from the west, what rays did you send forth again from the east! The great emperor was seized with disease, his body was so exhausted and weakened, not only by age, but also by various labors, that all soon began to suspect what had happened, and so much fear suddenly invaded the hearts of all, that it seemed that nothing could be more unworthy to suffer. Alas! how many prayers, how many supplications, how many wishes for his safety, or rather for the safety of the entire world, of all races, ages, and classes! There was no one who would rather die alive than live dead. Each one put his safety before his own: for they knew that their own safety belonged to each man, but that his safety was common to all mortals and to the whole world. For here he supported the whole world as if by some very firm pillar, and did not suffer himself to be shaken, harassed, or overthrown by any kind of storm; but with the equality of all the virtues with which he was endowed, he ruled in the midst of a firm and stable temperament. Oh, by what arts, by what labor he founded the empire, by what valor he strengthened and established liberty, by what clemency he increased the fortunes, peace, and happiness of his people! O excellent prince and admirable virtues, by which he excelled all others, prudence overcame the strong, by strength the wise, I should speak more correctly, he preceded the wise in counsel, the strong in strength. But no one was equal to his temperance. Justice is more eminent than all who have ever presided over the Roman Empire. Why should I remember his faith? what facility? what talent what excellent knowledge of all things? what liberality? What is the size of the mind? What is humanity, meekness, kindness? I weaken myself so wretchedly with tears and pain, that I cannot relate the excellency of his virtues because of excessive grief. We are now the most unfortunate people deprived of all these things. Alas! Not one nation, nor the people of one state, but all the Christians in the present, has done such a great slaughter! O miserable condition of men! O vain hope! O sweet once the name of empire! Oh, the freedom of Greece so often desired and sometimes restored! O inviolable law and most holy laws! Have you finally cut it all off? Ahem! Where have we arrived? Ahem! Where are we reduced to miseries and calamities? Now the senate is mourning, the princes are dying, all the provinces are lamenting, the cities are weeping, the municipalities are weeping, the colonies are in disrepair, the houses are afflicted, and finally the lands themselves seem to follow with sighs and tears and weeping a prince so meek, so pious, and so salutary. O time! so that, to the former evils, you had to add this last, and of all that we have ever suffered, the greatest and most unworthy? so as to obscure the fame and memory of the other evils by the greatness of this last one? Indeed, whatever adversities befell us before this, such as wars, conflicts, slaughters, plunders, and other things which were wont to follow from them, those divine wisdom of the emperor were ameliorated for the better. But now that we are left by him, who else can we seek refuge in, whom can we appeal to, whose protection can we implore? We have come to the extreme of all evils, we have become like orphans of a bereaved father, on whom our whole life depended, on whose constant labor we all experienced labor and led a very pleasant life. But Jain would rather die for us than live in such calamity and misery. Indeed, to live badly, as the poet says, is a laborious thing. O great and intolerable pain, which invaded all alike, and left no one untouched; no man, no woman, no young man, no old man! Oh, that gloomy and not at all desirable report, which spread here and there, roused all to the funeral of the most pious emperor! O most unhappy death of him on whose life the salvation of the world depended!

ON THE DEATH OF MANUEL II

O sighs, O tears, O sobs, O bitterest voices, O bitterest cries, O groans, O weeping, O mourning of all sex, age, order, condition! Some, indeed, sought a lord, others the father of the country, others the emperor, others the patron, others the teacher, others the founder of law and laws, but all of them who had become all things for all, as he says. O heavy and harsh contention among those who were present! Everyone strove to be seen as superior by weeping. The earth was ravaged by torrents of tears, and the funeral was carried by the hands of the nobles. From every place a multitude of citizens and foreigners flocked, filling the streets and filling the air and ether with pitiful groans. There was one voice of all, one cry, one groan. He, however, lay silent and dead, neither feeling what was going on, nor understanding the cries of the people. Nothing was to be seen but an empty corpse, and as if he had never been born, or had commanded nothing, or had not lived so many years, he was utterly destitute of every sense. He was indeed asked for the reason why he had wished to desist from us; for the answer was silence. Oh, the silence that is hated and least expected of us! Where is that language so learned, so sweet, from which speech sweeter than honey used to come out, with the movement of which everything seemed to resound, whose abundance opened up every question, resolved every doubt, in such a way that it taught everything, and so often aroused the hearers, that it was not so much persuasion as matter to put before his eyes, and not to set others on fire as much as he himself seemed to be burning? Whence now such a sudden silence? Why such a sudden change? Could the ferocity of death overcome you too, most excellent emperor, who saw the Atlantic Ocean in its danger for us, whom Italy looked upon, and which beyond Italy are the nations of the west? To whom, when you had gone to seek the favor of a garrison against the Barbarians, you were held in the greatest honor. From which we have easily seen that the strength of an empire is not contained in the multitude of funds, nor in the number of forces, but in the valor, moderation, and wisdom of the prince. O singular prudence, which the Latin men, and the most prudent by nature and experience of many things, received with astonishment and astonishment in the Peloponnese! Did he not also add the greatest part of Thessaly to his rule? He was equally active in arms and provided with counsel; for he had Thucydides with him, and Xenophon, and if there was any one like them, whose counsel he used continually, from which it was done that, as Homer says, he was both the best king and the strongest warrior. and what we are going to do is a very eloquent speaker. But where are all these now? Where is the applause, and preaching, and praise? Where did the people perceive that indescribable pleasure, which they perceived from the power, moderation, and clemency of the prince, so that, ruling that government, they seemed to themselves to be the happiest? You are the calmest of all things! Lo labored for us, as they were wont to do, by which, by using the nerves of his eloquence, he easily induced the Medes and Persians to take up arms against that impious emperor of the Turks, to whom, in a short time interposed, he was vanquished and punished for his crimes. Silently he overcame his enemies as often as he did without arms, by authority and prudence alone, which is the most beautiful kind of victory; How many cities, how many towns, and the situation and nature of the most fortified places, we enjoyed in the leisure of the court. Who will give us an emperor, who a father, who a patron, who a champion, who a teacher of manners and life, who a lord so beneficent and salutary? Let the Christian republic mourn now, whose most splendid eye has been extinguished. Let the earth now begin a plaintive song; the column by which it used to be supported fell down. All are now clothed in sackcloth and sprinkled with ashes. This calamity has no remedy. Who now holds the keys of such an empire, who can handle the governments of the whole world? O letter, weep for your worshiper. He has perished who raised you lying in the ashes and filth and brought you back as it were from darkness to light, who pursued you with such love, that neither public nor private affairs, nor cares or anxieties, nor any pleasure, nor sleep could distract him from your company. And just as he followed you with incredible diligence and diligence, so he excited the others to do the same; and not only the young, but also the old, he exhorted discipline. Whereupon it came to pass that most of those whose age was already advancing, moved by the example of the excellent emperor, transferred themselves to the study of the best arts. For it is thus arranged by nature, that such as the princes are, such also should be the subjects; and just as those whom princes abhor, are a sport to all, so those which they honor, are worshiped by all and held in high esteem. O laws, O judges, O forum, O seats, O tribunals, mourn the extinction of the priest who gave you that for the sake of the administration of justice and equity you may most justly inherit these names. O citizens and lords of the cities, you deserve the emperor who was taken away from you, who talked with you about all things with such ease and prudence! O poor people, weep for the patron who protected you, relieved you, fed you! O whatever is the blood of Greece, fill all, as you do, with tears and sorrow, and be deprived of your pilot, who protected you from every attack and tempest of fortune, and avert the storms of war that often threaten you, now with arms and with war, now only with prudence and authority. . In fact, this was characteristic of the wisest emperor in the first place, to be ignorant of neither time, nor measure, nor the arts of war and peace. I certainly think that even his enemies and enemies will pursue him to a great extent and join us in lamentations and in so heavy and bitter a mourning. All were conquered by the valor of the prince, whose strength is so great that he is honored even by his enemies. O Byzantium, Byzantium! Oh, the brightest light of these cities, the glory of the world, the harbor of the shipwrecked, the refuge of the miserable, the bulwark of all goods, what an emperor, what wisdom, piety, and clemency you have hitherto endowed! Who has restored to you your former liberty, wealth, fortunes, and dominion; who formerly subdued your enemies to you; who, besides these laws of peace, gave hope to all. Alas! What a pit you have now fallen into! Unhappy! It is a pity that you have lost that and the ornament which you had, the most beautiful of all. Where now is that golden caesarean of yours, where is the sight pleasing to all mortals? Alas! What kind of hair do you have? with what virtues the ungodly death has driven out those who were twisted! What an eye he took out, that he cut off the head, and left you semi-dead and half-dead, nay, completely dead and motionless! Alas! How wide and how spacious a field of tears and mourning has he proposed to you, not at all desirable to you. Nevertheless, it has been so, and you suffer these things; for what will you do, having thus spoken to God? We now stand as your children, dressed in pitiful attire, and beginning a plaintive song. Oh, the various and manifold discourses in his mind, as if arranged in some venerable inn, and thence flowing forth from a most abundant fountain! These indeed emphasized faith, piety, and religion; they decorated temples, sacrifices, and festivals; others debated about virtue and morals; some were attacked by their faults; most of them discussed what to do and what to avoid with incredible facility, splendor, and grace. There are those who stand as witnesses of that book, bearing before them the highest learning, singular genius, and divine wisdom, although he was far from being present to us wretched people, and he who preached to us is to be marveled at, what after the ashes of his writings of life, virtue, and manners we can conjecture. It is true that all have suffered a great loss, but we, who are still young, have lost such a man, almost before we know it. None allowed us to hear him pray more often, not to give applause to the preacher, not to offer him the fruits of our talent, whatever they were, before he departed from life. But now, we are forced to offer the first fruits of grief and tears and mourning to me, poor and unhappy. Alas! In what times we are reserved, how bitter a struggle for us, jealous death, you proposed! O calamities greater than all calamities that have ever been! How can we live longer! How can this unfortunate soul, whatever little life remains, be transported in so much grief and sorrow! Where he is now king, for us the ever-watchful eye, which sleep could never overcome, the ruler of all things, as Homer says. He stayed awake all night, either meditating on something or reading; he spent the day in conversation and business. Very good commander! How will you be able to endure so much leisure under this bitter stone, who, as if having wings, used to fly around the whole world? How could he bear so long a silence, whose speech, like the song of the Sirens, softened men's ears, and, like a mighty iron, he always drew wherever he pleased? It is true that you have departed, and having been called to better dwellings, you have migrated to heaven, where you had prepared for yourself a perpetual seat by faith, religion, and virtue. But why have you left us in so much mourning and sorrow and tears? Why didn't you call everyone to leave? For it would have been better to die with you than to live without you.

ON THE DEATH OF MANUEL II

LATIN TEXT

Si flere etiam aliquando fas est, et amaram socictatem constituere cantus atque doloris, non video quod tempus huic rei accommodari melius possit, quam præsens, in quo quidquid gaudii, Jatitiæ ac voluptatis erat, sublatum atque exstinctum est, et pro his successit dolor, mæstitia, gemitus. Quod nunc esse nobis solatium amplius potest, quæ melioris fortunæ spes, quod tantæ infelicitatis remedium? Tondeatur nunc orbis terrarum, mutent universi vestem, lugubrem omnes habitum sumant, et tam insignem calamitatem una voce deplorent. Neque enim mediocrem fecimus jacturam, nec malum passi sumus cui adhiberi remedium possit. Ablatus nobis est repente divus imperator, totius orbis terrarum decus; qui dono quodam Providentiæ rerum gubernacula susceperat, ut tranquillitatem, quietem, felicitatem omnibus præstaret; ut communis omnium pater esset; ut res humanæ dignitate et gloria florerent. Jamjam omnis fortuna mutata est: labuntur omnia in pejus et res ad pristinum statum redeunt. Me miserum! Quantum unius hominis interitu damnum res hu manæ fecerunt! Abiit ille atque excessit e vita: nobis nihil præter suspiria, et luctum, et lacrymas reliquit. Abstulit e nobis omnem lætitiam, abstulit felicitatem, abstulit libertatem, et quod omnium pulcherrimum erat, seipsum abstulit. Heu! quis adeo constans, vel durus potius, et vere adamantinus est, qui temperare a lacrymis possit; qui non et animo commoveatur, et toto corpore perhorreat; qui non quæritet defunctum, ac gemitu, si fieri possit, revocare in vitam contendat? Cur a nobis tam repente evolasti, piissime imperator? Cur manere nobiscum diutius noluisti? Cur regio ilo virtutum tuarum concentu frui nobis ultra non Ircun? Suscepisti de nobis hactenus omnem curam et ut ipsi tuti ac laboris expertes viveremus, tu solus maxime semper claborasti. Testantur hoc populi omnes; testantur omnes provinciæ; terra omnis et maria omnia testantur. Nunc vero bona omnia tecum ferens abiisti. Quæ jam nobis esse sine te vitæ jucunditas potest, vel potius quomodo vivere sine te amplius possumus, quasi corpora quibus sublatum sit caput? Mortui enim jam omnes videmur, et ad nihilum redacti sumus. Sol, qui terrarum opera fulgentibus radiis lustras, heu! Quam infaustum atque infelicem hunc diem nobis illucescere fecisti! Heu! Quam acerbum, indignum ac miserabile spectaculum ipse vidisti! Melius certe fuerat, te sub terris duntaxat errantem, in perpetuis nos tenebris relinquere, quam radiorum tuorum splendore illustrare superiores plagas ut infelicibus oculis bustum hoc cerneremus regii corporis, quod tot pro nobis labores, tot vigilias, tot pericula sæpe subierat. O quales radios occidens, quales rursus oriens emisisti! Correptus est morbo optimus imperator, corpus ejus ita non modo ætate, sed variis etiam laboribus, confectum ac debilitatum erat, ut suspicari mox omnes cœperint quod evenit, tantusque animos omnium repente metus invasit, ut nihil indignius esse ferendum videretur. Heu! quot preces, quot supplicationes, quot vota pro illius salute, vel potius pro totius orbis terrarum incolumitate omnium generum, ætatum, ordinum fuere! Nemo erat qui mori potius illo superstite, quam mortuo illo vivere amplius vellet. Salutem illius suæ quisque saluti anteponebat: sciebant namque singuli salutem suam ad singulos homines pertinere, illius vero incolumitatem omnium mortalium et totius orbis terrarum esse communem. Hic enim universum orbem quasi firmissima quædam columna sustinebat, nec labefactari, vexari, everti ullo procellæ genere patiebatur; sed æquo virtutum omnium, quibus præditus erat, temperamento firmum ac stabilem in medio regebat. O quibus artibus, quo labore fundavit imperium, qua virtute firmavit ac stabilivit libertatem, qua clementia auxit populorum suorum fortunas, quietem, felicitatem! O eximiæ principis admirabilesque virtutes, quibus omnibus omnes superabat, prudentia fortes vincebat, fortitudine prudentes, vei ut rectius loquar, consilio callidos, viribus robustos anteibat. Atqui temperantia nemo ei par fuit. Justitia omnibus, qui unquam Romano imperio præfuerunt, babitus est præstantior. Quid fidem ejus commemorem? quid facilitatem? quid ingenium? quid eximiam rerum omnium scientiam? quid liberalitatem? Quid animi magnitudinem? Quid humanitatem, mansuetudinem, comitatem? Me miserum ita lacrymis ac dolore debilitor, ut præ nimio mœrore referre virtutum ejus excellentiam non possim. His omnibus nunc infelicissimi hominum privati sumus. Heu! Quantamjacturam non una gens, nec unius civitatis populus, sed omne Christianorum genus in præsentia fecit! O misera hominum conditio! O spes inanes! O dulce quondam nomen imperii! O toties desiderata et aliquando restituta Græcis libertas! O jus inviolabile et sanctissimæ leges! Huccine tandem omnia recidistis? Hem! Quo pervenimus? Hem! Quo miseriarum et calamitatis redacti sumus? Luget nunc senatus, mœrent principes, provinciæ omnes queruntur, plorant urbes, flent municipia, squalent coloniæ, domus afflictantur, agri denique ipsi tam mansuetum, tam pium, tam salutarem principem suspiriis, et lacrymis, et fletu prosequi videntur. O tempus! siccine superioribus malis, ultimum hoc, et omnium, qua passi unquam fuimus, maximum atque indignissimum addere debebas? siccine cæterorum malorum famam ac recordationem postremi hujus magnitudine obscurare? Etenim quacunque nobis ante hoc adversa contingebant, utpote bella, conflictus, cædes, spolia et alia quæ ex iis sequi consueverunt divina illa imperatoris sapientia emendabantur in melius. Nunc autem ab illo relicti, quem alium kabemus ad quem confugere, quem appellare, cujus præsidium implorare possumus? Deventum est al extrema malorum omnium, facti sumus quasi pupilli orbati patre, a quo nostro omnis vita pendebat, cujus assiduo labore omnis nos laboris expertes vitam ducebamus amoenissimanı. Jain vero longe nobis emori præstaret, quam in tanta calamitate et miseria vivere. Etenim male vivere, ut poeta inquit, laboriosa res est. O magnum atque intolerabilem dolorem, qui omnes pariter invasit, et neminem reliquit intactum; nou virum, non mulierem, non juvenem, non senem! O lugubrem illam famam ac minime optabilem quæ passim pervagata omnes ad funus piissimi imperatoris excitabat! O infelicissima mors illius cujus in vita salus orbis terrarum nitebatur! O suspiria, O lacrymæ, O singultus, O voces acerbissimæ, o amarissimi clamores, o gemitus, o fletus, o luctus omnis sexus, ætatis, ordinis, conditionis! Alii quidem dominum quærebant, alii patrem patriæ, alii imperatorem, alii patronum, alii magistrum, alii juris et legum conditorem, omnes vero eum, qui pro omnibus, ut ille inquit, omnia factus erat. O gravis atque aspera inter eos qui aderant contentio! Certabat quisque ut fletu superior videretur. O lacrymarum torrentibus obruta tellus ferebatur funus procerum manibus. Undecunque vero civium atque exterorum multitudo coufluebat, implentes vias et miserabili gemitu aerem atque æthera complentes. Una omnium vox, unus clamor, unus gemitus erat. Iste vero silens ac mortuus jacebat, nec quæ gerebantur sentiens, nec hominum clamores intelligens. Nihil præter inane cadaver conspiciebatur, et quasi natus unquam non fuisset, aut nunguam imperasset, aut tot annos non vixisset, prorsus omni sensu erat destitutus. Petebatur quidem ab eo ratio cur nos descrere voluisset; pro responso silentium erat. O taciturnitatem invisam et a nobis minime exspectatam! Ubi est lingua illa tam erudita, tam suavis, ex qua melle dulcior exire oratio solebat, cujus motu omnia tonare videbantur, cujus ubertas omnem aperiebat quæstionem, omne dubium solvebat, ita vero docebat cuncta, ita sæpenumero auditores excitabat, ut non tam suadere quam rem ante oculos ponere, nec tam accendere alios quam ipse ardere videretur? Unde nunc tam repentinum silentíum? Unde tam subita mutatio? An te quoque, optime imperator, superare mortis sævitia potuit, quem Atlanticum pelagus pro nobis periclitantem vidit, quem Italia aspexit, et quæ ultra Italiam sunt occiduæ gentes? Ad quas cum petendi adversus Barbaros præsidii gratia profectus fuisses, maximo in honore habitus fuisti. Ex quo facile perspeximus non pecuniarum multitudine , non copiarum numero robur imperii contineri, sed virtute , moderatione ac sapientia principis. O prudentia singularis, quam

Latini homines, et natura et multarum rerum experientia prudentissimi, admirari ac stuper Peloponneso recepit! Nonne etiam maximam Thessaliæ partem imperio suo adjecit? Idem et armis strenuus erat, et consilio providus; habebat enim Thucydidem secum, et Xenophontem, et si quis his similis erat, quorum consilio continuo utebatur ex quo fiebat ut, quemadmodum inquit Homerus, et rex optimus esset et bellator fortissimus. et quod nos adimus, facundissimus orator. At ubi nunc hæc omnia sunt? Ubi plausus, et præconia, et laudes? Ubi populorum ineffabilis illa voluptas, quam ex principis virtute, moderatione, clementia, tantam percipiebant, ut, illo imperium regente, beatissimi sibi esse viderentur? O summa rerum tranquillitas! Lo pro nobis laborante, sce solebant, qua adhibitis eloquentiæ suæ nervis, facile Medos et Persas induxit, ut adversus impium illum Turcarum imperatorem arma capesserent, quibus illc parvo interjecto tempore, victus ac profligatus debitas scelerum suorum poenas luit. Taceo quoties sine armis, sola auctoritate et prudentia, quod pulcherrimum victoriæ genus est, hostes superavit, quamque armis quoque quando res ferret, ita utebatur, ut merito et fortissimus et rei militaris peritissimus haberetur. Quot urbes nuper, quot oppida, et situ et natura locorum munitissima, in curi otio fruebamur. Quis nobis modo imperatorem reddet, quis patrem, quis patronum, quis propugnatorem, quis morum et vitæ magistrum, quis dominum tam beneficum et salutarem? Lugeat nune Christiana respublica, cujus splendidissimus oculus exstinctus est. Incipiat jam terra flebilem cantum; columna corruit qua sustentari solebat. Omnes nunc saccum induant et cinere spargantur. Remedium non habet ista calamitas. Quis nunc claves tanti imperii tenere, quis tractare totius orbis gubernacula poteri? O litteræ, plorate cultorem vestrum. Periit ille qui vos in coeno et sordibus jacentes erexit et quasi e tenebris ad lucem revocavit; qui tanto vos amore prosequebatur, ut nec publica nec privata negotia, nec curæ aut sollicitudines, nec voluptas aliqua nec somnus distrahere eum a vestro consortio posset. Et quemadmodum vos incredibili studio ac diligentia sequebatur, ita cæteros, ut idem facerent, excitabat; nec adolescentes duntaxat, verum etiam senes ad disciplinam hortabatur. Quo factum est, ut plerique quorum ætas jam ingravescens erat, exemplo optimi imperatoris permoti, ad optimarum artium studia se transtulerint. Sic enim natura comparatum est, ut quales sunt principes, tales etiam subditi fiant; et quemadmodum ca a quibus principes abhorrent, omnibus ludibrio sunt, ita quæ illi honorant, coluntur ab omnibus et in pretio habentur. O leges, O judices, O forum, O subsellia, O tribunalia, lugete exstinctum priuci pem qui vobis tribuerat ut propter justitiæ et æquitatis administrationem hæc nomina justissime possideretis. O cives et urbium optimates, mærete ablatum vobis imperatorem, qui tanta facilitate et prudentia vobiscum de rebus omnibus loquebatur! O pauperes, flete patronum qui vos protegebat, sublevabat, alebat! O quidquid Græci sanguinis usquam est, omnia, ut facitis, lacrymis ac moerore complete, cum vestro gubernatore privati sitis, qui vos ab omni impetu et procella fortunæ tuebafur, et minantes sæpe bellorum turbines nunc armis et bello, nunc sola prudentia atque auctoritate avertel at. Etenim hoc in primis sapientissimi imperatoris proprium erat, nec tempus, nec moduin, nec artes belli et pacis ignorare. Hunc profecto opinor etiam hostes atque inimicos ejus magna ex parte prosequi, ac lamentis, et in tam gravi atque acerbo luctu nobiscum misceri. Vicit omnes principis virtus, cujus tanta vis est, ut etiam ab hostibus honoretur. O Byzantium, Byzantium! O Hium urbium clarissimum lumen, decus orbis terrarum, naufragorum portus, miserorum perfugium, præsidium omnium bonorum, qualem imperatorem, quanta sapientia, pietate, clementia præditum hactenus habuisti! Qui tibi pristinam libertatem, diguitatem, fortunas, imperium restituit; qui hostes tuos dominari antea solitos, tibi subjecit; qui pacis cis leges præter spem omnium dedit. Heu! In quantas nunc ærumnas incidisti! Infelix! Amisisti decus illud atque ornamentum, quod omnium pulcherrimum habebas. Ubi nunc est tua illa aurea cæsaries, ubi mortalibus omnibus gratus aspectus? Heu! Quales tibi crines. quibus virtutibus intortos impia mors evulsit! Qualem oculum abstulit, quod caput abscidit, et te seminecem ac semimortuam, imo vero mortuam prorsus atque immobilem reliquit! Heu! Quam latum et quam spatiosum campum tibi proposuit lacrymarum et luctus, minime quidem tibi optabilem. Verumtamen ita factum est, et tu ista pateris; quid enim facere poies, Deo ita jabente? Stamus nunc tui filii, miserabilem induti habitum, et flebilem cantum inchoantes. O varii multiplicesque sermones in animo illius, quasi in venerabili quodam diversorio dispositi, et inde velti ex abundantissimo fonte manantes! Hi quidem fidem, pietatem, religionem extollebant; illi templa, sacrificia, dies festos ornabant; alii de virtute et moribus disputabant; nonnulli vitia insectabantur; plerique, quid agendum, quid vitandum esset, incredibili facilitate, splendore, gratia, disserebant. Testes sunt, qui exstant illius libri, summam doctrinam, singulare ingenium et divinam sapientiam præ se ferentes, quanquam infelicibus nobis longe præstaret vivum illum, ac concionantem admirari, quam post cineres ex illius scriptis vitæ, et virtutis, et morum facere conjecturam. Magnam certe jacturam omnes fecerunt, sed nos in primis qui adhuc adolescentes talem virumi, prius fere quam nosse possumus, amisimus.

Non licuit nobis orantem sæpius audire, non concionanti plausum reddere, non illi priusquam e vita discederet, primitias ingenii nostri qualescunque essent, offerre. Nunc vero, me miserum atque infelicem mæroris et lacrymarum et luctus offerre primitias cogimur. Heu! In quæ tempora reservati sumus, quam amarum nobis certamen, mors invida, proposuisti! O clades omnibus quæ unquam fuerunt cladibus major! Quomodo vivere amplius poterimus! Quomodo infelicem hanc animam, quantulumcunque vitæ supersit, in tanto luctu ac mœrore traducere! Ubi nunc est regius ille pro nobis semper pervigil oculus quem nunquam vincere somnus poterat, rerum, ut Homerus inquit, omnium domitor. Vigilabat ille noctes totas, aut meditans aliquid, aut legens; dies in sermonibus atque negotiis consumebat. Optime imperator! Quomodo sustinere sub hoc amaro lapide tantum otium poteris, qui quasi pennas habens, circumvolitare totum orbem solebas? Quomodo tam diuturnum silentium ferre, cujus oratio, quasi cantus Sirenum, demulcebat hominum aures, et quasi magnes ferrum, quocunque vellet, semper trahebat? Verum tu quidem abiisti, et ad meliora habitacula vocatus migrasti in cœlum, ubi perpetuam sedem fide, religione, virtute tibi paraveras. Nos autem cur in tanto luctu et moerore, et lacrymis reliquisti? Cur discedens omnes non vocasti? Mori enim tecum quam sine te vivere commodius fuisset.

The Scriptorium Project is the work of a small group of lay people of various apostolic churches who are interested in the preservation, transmission, and translation of the works of the early and medieval church. Our efforts are to make the works of the church fathers accessible to anyone who might have an interest in Christian antiquities and the theological, philosophical, and moral writings that have become the bedrock of Western Civilization.

To-date, our releases have pulled from the Greek, Syriac, Georgian, Latin, Celtic, Ethiopian, and Coptic traditions of Christianity, and have been pulled from sundry local traditions and languages.

ON THE DEATH OF MANUEL II

Other Selections from the Byzantine Church Series:

Funeral Oration for Bessarion by Michael Apostolius (Mar. 2007)
Treatise on Sobriety by Nicephorus the Solitary (Apr. 2007)
Sermons by Nestorius of Constantinople (May 2009)
On the Death of Manuel II by John Bessarion (June 2010)
Theophrastus by Aeneas of Gaza (Apr. 2011)
Treatise on Prayer by St. Evargius of Ponticus (May 2011)
The Lausiac History by St. Palladius of Galatia (Mar. 2013)
Letter on the Fall of Constantinople by Isidore of Kiev (Oct. 2013)
The Hesychast by Gregory of Sinai (June 2015)
Selected Laws by Justinian I, Emperor of Rome (July 2018)
Exhortation to Monks Ordained in India by St. John of Karpathos (March 2021)
Fragments of 'Chronicle' by Hippolytus of Thebes (May 2023)
The Life of the Blessed Theotokos by Epiphanius Monachus (July 2023)
Letters of Nestorius by Nestorius of Constantinople (Sept. 2023)

ON THE DEATH OF MANUEL II